Endorsements

"Often the things we resist the most fiercely are the very things we require for true growth and progress. We may never tap into the power of our potential if we don't push through the process of recognizing our limitations to discover a greater magnitude of strength. So many of us are looking to eliminate pressure from our lives, but my friend Sam Beckworth highlights the value of pressure as a tool for transformation. Opening your heart and mind to the perspective he puts forth can help you see vulnerability and weakness in a whole new paradoxical light."

—Paul Loeffler, Radio, TV Broadcaster

"The demands of business can become toxic. Sam does a tremendous job teaching us to press into the pressure we all face, so that we can handle what the corporate world throws our way with a better understanding and greater skill."

—Michael Graef, CFP, Founding Partner at Inspire Investing

"As a human resources professional, I really relate to the transparency aspect of this book. Many of us H.R. leaders make decisions with other business executives behind closed doors and then only share the outcome and result of that corroboration. However, I've found when there is transparency as to why the decision was made and who contributed to those decisions, this is normally better received by employees."

Cherrity Ricks, Society of Human Resources
Management Kern Chapter Conference Chair

"An amazing blueprint for finding inner-strength and fulfillment. Sam has provided a solid guideline for personal development that can improve both business and personal relationships. An essential read."

—Brian Icenhower, CEO and Founder of
Icenhower Coaching, Real Estate Industry Leader

"All of us are hard wired to resist pressure. Yet, pressure is designed to bring out the best in us, not the worst. In *A Friend Named Pressure*, Sam Beckworth dissects both the burden and blessing of pressure in a profoundly effective way. If you want to cut to the chase, and unpack the riddle of how to use the pressures of life to bring about exceptional results, this book is an easy read about a hard topic."

—Francis Anfuso, Author and Speaker,
KLOVE Radio Devotionals

"I really enjoyed this book. It's rare that someone writes about the value of small victories and true vulnerability. These days it seems that everyone wants to lead but not many will pay the price of to lead with with vulnerability. Sam communicates this with eloquence. The book is also interlaced with the author's personal stories and humor which make it an easy read. I recommend this book for anyone that manages people."

—Bryan Sutherland, Founder & CEO,
Vision Guitar, San Jose

"As a police force veteran, I really needed this book. We are all often faced with pressure daily, whether it is from work, family, or other life obligations. They can be overwhelming and crippling to those who have not figured out how to manage it. Sam reminds us through historical figures, pop culture, and his own personal journey, that pressure, when wielded properly, can be overcome and used positively for one's success and personal victories.

Sam takes us through concrete steps of understanding the challenges presented by pressure and gives suggestions, including biblical inspiration, which I personally use to help guide me through my struggles of pressure."

—Teddy Aguirre, Sergeant, LAPD

A Friend Named
PRESSURE

Going from Weakness to Strength

SAM BECKWORTH

Published by Freiling Agency, LLC.

P.O. Box 1264
Warrenton, VA 20188

www.FreilingAgency.com

ISBN: 979-8-9881634-6-6
eBook ISBN: 979-8-9881634-7-3

Printed in the United States of America

Table of Contents

"Their weakness was turned to strength."

Hebrews 11:34

1

Understanding Limitations and Personal Capacity

The Essence of Weakness

I was caught up to paradise and heard things so astounding that they cannot be expressed in words, things no human is allowed to tell. So to keep me from becoming proud, I was given a thorn in my flesh, a messenger from Satan to torment me. Three different times I begged the Lord to take it away. Each time he said, "My grace is all you need. My <u>power works best in weakness</u>."
St. Paul (2 Corinthians 12:4–9, NLT)

RELIGIOUS OR NOT, many would agree Saul of Tarsus, better known as the Apostle Paul, remains a giant among the greats in human history. His accomplishments, leadership strengths, and message reverberate to this day. Paul perplexed hell, changed societies and economies, brought down one the seven wonders of the ancient world, out-hustled every one of his contemporaries, did the common things, performed the supernatural, and effectively became the greatest salesman in the world by writing a hefty portion of the best-selling book in human history.

Yet, he still had a broken human nature just like everyone else. Paul was spent, begged for his circumstances to change, and faced excruciating opposition in his particular race. We see a man with identifiable challenges and questions. Yet ultimately, he went from a position of overwhelming weakness to one of an unstoppable force. In Paul's experiences, we will find some of our own struggles and draw practical strength for our everyday life.

As brilliant and unrelenting as this great leader was, we are first going to start our journey on a more practical side of things. Paul wrestled with the essence of something all humanity deals with: *weakness.*

Weakness is a big word and we'll define it as we go along. In the greater sense, and in the most practical applications, weakness has to do with mankind's fallible human nature. It includes all manner of shortcomings, inferiority, disease of soul and body, addiction, failure, and all self-defeating behaviors.

Weakness is further defined as *to be without strength, feeble and inadequate.* Weakness is a *fault, malady, frailty and an unwholesome condition.* Weakness is to be *lacking in ... resources.*

Let's say someone's weakness is in their attitude; such as, control, perfectionism, or anger. Then on a difficult day, the familiar winds of adverse circumstances begin to blow, and soon this person falters in the direction of their weakness. They simply do not possess or demonstrate enough strength to resist that particular struggle.

This brings me to my personal definition of weakness, which is *an inadequate resistance against an unhealthy pressure.* Whatever the weakness, our personal resistance is insufficient against something hurtful, and occurs when one's resistance to that unique pressure falls short of making the better choice.

For now, let's focus not so much on the specific *malady*, but rather the *process* of becoming weak; not the *noun* of weakness but the *verb* of growing weak.

For example, three women live under the same roof as I do. I have a wife, two college-age daughters, and a neutered male Weiner dog. My three females are all strong. So, when they have PMS and periods at the same time, this can create estrogen driven turbulence. Heightened emotions create a tension that can drain a male's emotional resources.

Since a man is not born with a compass that guides him to healthy emotional connection with himself and others, there comes a time when a man hits his limits in that environment. Whether it is for a length of ten minutes or three days, every guy has a limited capacity of emotional resources. When his limit is met, he is capped out. When operating on empty, the dominant attitude in his behavior can become disconnection, passivity, or anger.

"It's not about the mountains we conquer, but ourselves."
—Sir Edmund Hilary

This is what we're getting at through this chapter. Your strength has limits and your soul has a capacity. These will tell you when you're maxed, done, lost your traction, reached your end, and your ability to do much good is gone. At this point, some have a meltdown, a breakdown, a showdown, or fall down on their crown, but most everyone has a frown.

So, for these first few chapters, as tough as it may be, I'll try to remove the negative stigma of weakness;

such as, feeling like a loser because of a lack of discipline. Instead, for now let's see weakness as a gauge, as a strength measurement, an identifiable place where one's resources end, and therefore discover the starting point for growth.

The gas gauge on an old car I used to have was faulty. Since I didn't know how much fuel was actually in my tank, I intentionally reset the trip mileage by my odometer so I would know when I needed to refill. I knew the size of the fuel tank and the approximate miles driven before it required a refill.

If I was driving fast in and out of city traffic, then I could burn through fuel more quickly than I would if I was just driving on the freeway for a few hours. Obviously, if I'm doing a lot of stop and go driving in town then I have less efficient gas mileage. I would need to compensate by refueling sooner regardless of the number of miles driven. I once drove 260 miles before I refilled, and when I did, I actually still had four gallons of gas left in my tank. Another time I drove 216 miles, and I ran out of gas, inconveniencing my wife and friends by having them bring me a gas can. I ended up refueling that tank around every 200 miles, regardless.

Some pressures pull from your capacity more than others. Whatever your situation, it is wise to keep better track and pay closer attention. However, there's something else that is very important.

• Look to extend your limitations and expand your capacity

Paul's Mentor spoke to him about the value of weakness. It is the doorway that leads to ability beyond our own. So, when you're "DONE," you're really not done. When you can't take it anymore, you can take more. When you get rigid and pouty and no longer flexible, there's an ability to be stretched beyond what you ordinarily would. When you get uncomfortable and inclined to trigger with control to those in your circle, there is an ability to remain in that environment with composure a little longer before you act out.

We can go from weakness to strength. Your personal limitations are the starting point. It leads to the quality nutrients only found in the breakfast plate called, Adversity. Instead of all of your problems disappearing, there is explosive strength at the place of your limitation.

"You are never really playing an opponent. You are playing yourself, your own highest standards, and when you reach your limits, that is real joy."

—Arthur Ashe

2

Understanding the Value of Pressure

It Can Work for You

"In the world you will have <u>tribulation</u> (pressure)…"
—The Mentor - (John 16:33)

"For our light <u>affliction </u>(pressure), which is but for a moment, is working for us…"
—The Mentee - (2 Corinthians 4:17)

PRESSURE IS INEVITABLE. There is no escape. This is a foundational fact so it's best to embrace it. *Thlipsis,* the Greek word used here, translates simply as *pressure.* The word is used for crushing grapes or olives in a press In order for us to flip adversity to our advantage, we will need to understand the value of pressure. Even though most of the time it doesn't feel very good, pressure works for us.

Saul faced excessive difficulties walking out his vision. These abnormal beatings were stoked by an unseen spiritual enemy to create pressure specifically to slow him down or stop him from communicating to the world the Good News he received from the King. Paul was extremely effective and, as a consequence, faced some excrutiating backlash of his own.

Let's see what Paul went through:

- put in prison…often
- whipped times without number
- faced death again and again
- suffered thirty-nine lashes five different times
- beaten with rods three times
- stoned (with literal rocks)
- shipwrecked three times
- spent a whole night and a day adrift at sea
- traveled on many long journeys
- faced threats from robbers
- faced danger from his own people, the Jews, as well as from the Gentiles

- faced danger in the cities, in the deserts, and on the seas
- faced multiple betrayals
- worked hard and long, enduring many sleepless nights
- often without food, hungry, and thirsty
- shivered in the cold, without enough clothing to keep him warm

Because of all of this, Paul said, "*I was pressed (Thlipsis) beyond measure.*" And yet, this same guy was the one who explained that this pressure is *working for us.* Since Paul has the experience and credibility to advise us on this, what value then does pressure have? Among many things, pressure helps in the following ways.

Pressure Draws Weakness to the Surface

Pressure helps us become aware of what's troubling us and others about us. Pressure brings inadequacies front and center. We might try to bury it, deny it, explain it, confess it away but pressure has a way keeping weaknesses in our face. Paul's limitations became something he could no longer ignore. He wanted God just to stop the whole thing.

Weakness can also pose a danger if left unchecked. If an excessive food appetite is a weakness, then ignoring the lack of resistance can lead to a number of problems. We can get sick, spend money on copayments and procedures, get sluggish and spend less time with the family, and hurt ourselves and those we love. Thankfully, pressure can keep weakness and its negative affects at the surface of our lives to such an agitating degree that we might consistently do something about it.

Pressure Reveals Our Limitations and Capacity

Pressure shows what we can and cannot handle. Pressure's testing aids us in discerning where we may have leaks in our soul to handle certain flows of life's pressure.

If you're familiar with the Marvel movie *The Avengers*, then you might be able to identify with the scene where Dr. Banner angrily and unknowingly picked up Loki's scepter in the presence of the other Avengers. The first time I saw the movie, I thought he was going to blow up and go green right there. Instead, he regained some composure and put the stick of destiny back on the counter.

If your weakness is anger, then there's a point where you can go from Dr. Banner to the Hulk. Your sanity flat lines. However, there's always a strategic moment of opportunity in between where you pick up the scepter and can still exercise self-control. Your moment might last only three seconds, but it is still an opportunity. Your pressured circumstances are working to help see where you need help.

Pressure Breaks Down in Order to Build Up

There's a term in weight training called *lifting to failure*. It is recommended by most experts for muscle development. Simply put, lifting to failure is described as selecting a weight amount that is heavy enough so that the last repetition taxes you to the point at which you can no longer physically complete it.

If you hit the ground right now and did as many pushups as you physically could until you could not perform the final pushup, you employed this principle of muscle failure. If you did six pushups but on the seventh your arms were wobbling and you couldn't complete it, then your "failure" pushup number was seven. Your resistance against the pressure of your body weight reveals what you could and could not do.

In order for muscles to grow, they must first break down. The science of muscle growth is first tearing. Now that you know your failure bench press, curl, squat, exercise, push up, you can go to failure again a couple of days later. You will probably find that your failure number has increased. Your muscles grew in strength first by their breaking down. It sounds a bit backwards, but we get stronger in pushing to failure.

> "The F-18 natops. It contains everything they want you to know about your aircraft. I'm assuming you know the book inside and out. So does your enemy. But what the enemy doesn't know is your limits. I intend to find them, test them, push beyond."
> —Maverick

Weights, resistance bands, relational tension, financial struggles, bouts of depression and worthlessness, ebbs and flows of a sense of inadequacy, irritating people, fears on the outside and inside, all flow within life's turbulent current called pressure. Pressure pushes you. But you can often push back enough with some determination, so that you find your emotional core is swelling a bit and growing in strength.

Pressure Transforms

Pressure transforms. Butterflies, pearls, and diamonds are in part the fruit of pressure. Pressure produces perseverance in us as we allow it enough time to harvest its benefits. It can also be a wrecking ball to stubborn things in our lives that won't move any other way.

This concept is helpful to a husband who genuinely wants to learn to connect emotionally with his wife. He is probably a pretty good guy but just can't connect well in her assessment, which is, by the way, the only one that really matters. He's like a frozen stick of butter to soft and warm, flaky bread. He's made of the right substance but not in the ideal form. He's trying to butter her up, but instead he's ripping and tearing her heart. His un-tempered engagement needs to be softened. Pressure thaws him to expand both his capacity and quality. Pressure aids this process, turning solid into liquid. Soft, melted butter to some warm fresh bread can make for a pretty good combination.

Pressure Generates Inconvenience

Pressure is offensive. Pressure provokes. Pressure agitates and is an inconvenience to the laziness and self-indulgence of our human nature. The Son of Man said although the *"spirit is willing, ... the flesh is weak"* (Matthew 26:41, NKJV).

Pressure forcefully demands a response. Pressure is an action that demands a reaction, and yet many are not inconvenienced enough to seek growth. We can all dodge life's pressure and cater to what our comfort and insecurities prefer. That's our choice. But very few will ever change without the inconvenience of pressure. Some are lukewarm while others are lazy. Pressure will either violently bury us or scare us out of our minds enough to rise up for something greater.

People in droves are trying to avoid pressure! They either try to move away from it, hope it stops, wonder if they've done something wrong to face it, or think it's evil without any redemptive opportunities. They misinterpret this gift. When we embrace it and are affected by it willingly, we grow.

Sadly, far too many avoid this universal gym at all costs. The monthly dues for not going are much higher than going.

To those whose flesh is weaker than their spirit, pressure intimidates and irritates. This is a sign you're going the wrong way and sleeping through your opportunity to grow and help others. You can grow through pressure or get fat and foggy in your head by sleeping through it all.

When Paul's Mentor was sweating and praying, Peter was sleeping because of some serious depression over what was happening. Pressure has that affect if we let it overrun us. He woke up to a scary scene and reacted. He was completely unprepared and cut a guy's ear off in an attempt to help the situation. Peter's stature shrunk, home-boy's ear got bloody dunked, Peter's self-worth sunk, his self-willed flesh added another chubby chunk, and then his wrong response to pressure turned him back into a fishing punk.

Remember, your friend named Pressure is working for you. Work together with it!

"When everything seems to be going against you,
remember that the airplane takes off
against the wind, not with it."

—Henry Ford

3

Understanding the Value of Process

Unpopular but Necessary

"What is measured can be managed."
—Peter Drucker

MANAGING GROWTH OFTEN calls for a process. Whether one is trying to lose weight, generate more sales, or start a new business, someone somewhere has already developed a blueprint of some sort to pattern your efforts after. The wheel need not be reinvented.

My wife attempted to lose weight for around ten years. The amount of effort, the money spent, the frustration and eventual depression was real. We've all witnessed or perhaps have been the one who began a new diet one day, and the next day got upset, ate an apple fritter and told people the new plan just didn't work. But that was certainly not the case here. It seemed to be an abnormal lack of success despite a desperate, ongoing, and painstaking effort.

However, through not giving up, she simply found the model that worked specifically for her. Pre-done meals that helped her mentally. Healthy nutrition that worked for her body. Satisfying food that was enjoyable and made her full. Measured macro-micro nutrients that moved her metabolism towards weight loss. This turnkey, tested method of a lifestyle change produced in my wife a weight loss of forty pounds in seven months through right nutrition and exercise. Her real key to success was a process: a preset model, prepared meals, and pre-measured nutrients. Her discipline easily handled the rest.

> *"Goals are good for setting a direction but systems are best for making progress."*
> —James Clear, *Atomic Habits*

We have a ruler, a plum line, a compass, a weight scale, a check register, a mirror, a level, a calendar. All of these are forms of measurement to help us understand where we are in order to manage a better result. So, find a model to aid your growth. Focus on the process, and the outcomes often take care of themselves.

You may have to tweak some things to suit you specifically, but someone else went ahead of you to birth a plan and chart a followable course. Find it. This is by no means an exhaustive blueprint here but as it's been said, "Go as far as you can go, and when you get there, you will see farther." The truth is, we only deserve to see farther if we're willing to go as far as we can go.

So, don't just join a gym. Hire a trainer. Don't just start a business. Hire a consultant. Don't necessarily jump into full-time self-employed sales. Consider becoming an employee for a sales organization and get excellent training and learn their model. We have *YouTube*, *Google*, digital courses, *LinkedIn* training, conferences, free content, templates and all kinds of access to tested systems for our benefit. Without fail, your efforts will attract even greater help.

Small Tweaks Led to Big Peaks

Social scientist, best-selling author, and TED speaker, Amy Cuddy said years ago that small tweaks lead to big changes. Adjustments to a process are necessary. By slightly changing the grip on a dumbbell, you can focus more precisely on a given part of your chest, shoulder, or bicep muscle. By adjusting one's fingers on a softball's threads, a pitcher can throw either a four-seam rising fast-ball, or a two-seam fastball that has sharp movement. Stay flexible. The focus is small improvements toward growth.

"Value the process more than events."
—John Maxwell

Twenty years ago, I had a desire to make a lot more money. It certainly wasn't my only desire and it wasn't the highest of my dreams. I did, however, have a sales process for prospecting, a CRM (customer relationship management) database for tracking, warm leads, and energy. I had a weekly sales meeting where I heard what my colleagues were doing in their book of business, phone calls made, referrals received, how many first, second and third appointments, sales, and commissions made the week prior. I had a process. My income grew by 50% nearly overnight.

As I thought about what more I could do, I read this quote by Henry David Thoreau:

"...if one advances confidently in the direction of his dreams, and endeavors to live the life which he has imagined, he will meet with a success in uncommon hours."

So, I added a simple adjustment to my plan. I decided to make sure I would stay at my office until my day was over. I wouldn't leave early. Simple, but it was a real temptation for all of us back then. One day shortly after committing to this, I was startled at the sound of someone knocking on my office window, which is something that never happened before. It was an existing client trying to get some new business done before he went out of town on one of his many vacations. He refused to wait until he got back, so we helped him and were compensated generously. Why? I simply tweaked an existing process and was rewarded for it in ways I had not expected.

Don't Get Too Cute

Look at Paul's successful pattern. He followed the words of the Master Carpenter: go out in all the world and say what I said and do what I did. He had the patterns of his more experienced contemporaries, the understanding of his Mentor through personal experience, his ancient writings, and the unstoppable motivation of his desire.

If anyone could have relied solely on his education, background, breeding, and smarts, it was Paul. Yet, he reduced himself to follow that simple model: Go and tell. It wasn't fancy but it was potent. There was a method to the madness of his life.

As a fruitful consequence, he was given a more complete and detailed model in his letters for other salesmen to follow. He wrote a thorough pattern of New Testament doctrine that makes the effectiveness of this message even more measurable for those in his trade today. His movement in honoring the basic vision brought the motherlode of greater insight.

Listen, if the devil is in the details, then we should be more so, as long as it makes our movement effective instead of giving us paralysis. For the Christians who are waiting for fire from heaven to fall, please consider that the Tabernacle under Moses and the Temple under Solomon had no fire until they first followed the detailed process given to them. Moses was given a tedious pattern to build and David was given a specific blueprint for the temple his son eventually built. These two ancient structures served their purpose and facilitated relationship and worship with their God.

So, if you're selling the Gospel like Paul did and you find yourself waiting for the supernatural to fall, if you're a salesman waiting for the phone to ring, if you're out of shape waiting for Richard Simmons to personally train you, if you have dreams without plans and goals, then save yourself frustration. Start looking for a process that will get you moving in the right direction, help you gain some traction, and give you a measurable roadmap to invest your efforts. Look for one that has a proven track record of the results you want and then jump into the workflow.

The Main Thing Is Keeping the Main Thing the Main Thing

Be old school in ethic and principle, but not necessarily in method. Twenty-five years ago, we were cold calling and knocking on doors. Now we have *LinkedIn*, email analytics, better workflows, metrics, updated sales pipelines, scaling methods, modern lead generation, effective CRMs like Salesforce, in order to enhance the sales experience and generate a warmer prospecting pool.

If your goal is greater sales revenue, then it wouldn't be helpful to engage primarily in door-to-door marketing when the methods of communication have improved so drastically. Just make your process serve the goal, not the other way around. As it's been said, implement then perfect.

> *"You must build this Tabernacle and its furnishings*
> *exactly according to the pattern I will show you."*
> —Exodus 25:8,9,40

4

Understanding the Value of Progress

Respecting Slow Growth

"Ease is a greater threat to progress than hardship."
—Denzel Washington

SOMETIMES GROWTH SEEMS too little and takes too long, but a good process will lead to respectable progress.

If you lose two pounds in one month, that is success. If you reduced your body fat by one-half percent, well done! Did you save $1,000? Great job. You may feel you could have done better, but if you focus on what you didn't lose, you'll get frustrated about that over a Costco chocolate cake and whipped cream. Don't sabotage your progress by underestimating what real progress is.

The better the process, the better you can recognize your progress, be encouraged by it, and build on it. Are you not changing fast enough for you? Are others not changing fast enough for you? Are circumstances not changing fast enough for you? Well, if there is a measure of progress, then there is proof of a positive direction. See it, respect it and expand it.

"Do not despise these small beginnings."
—Zechariah 4:10

As you value a measure of progress, even though it wasn't enormous in your eyes, you will begin to....

• Reach your limitations more quickly and often.

Since some growth comes through understanding the value of pressure, process, and progress, we can then intentionally reach and extend our limitations and capacity more quickly.

Test your limits. Challenge your weakness. Max your capacity. Spend the emotional resources left in your tank. Empty yourself. Give what you have. Overcome the negative with good.

• Reach your limitations through *proactive movement* rather than *involuntary circumstances.*

Go to the gym before it comes to you. Call your clients to see if you can help them with anything before they call you with a bunch of problems. Don't sit back in anxiety waiting for that dreaded weakness to come knocking on your door. Don't allow pressure to bully you. Use it and begin to push before it pushes you. It is more advantageous to act preemptively than to get

> *"Success is a journey, not a destination. The doing is often more important than the outcome."*
> —Arthur Ashe

cornered and react. David ran to meet Goliath. Then, he took the giant's head off. Get there first. Eat it for breakfast before it gets shoved down your throat!

• Challenge the pressure instead of allowing the pressure to stop you.

Paul told his Mentor to *please make the pressure stop because it's trying to stop me*! Yet, after receiving more accurate insight to his situation, he used adversity for his own growth instead of allowing it to compromise the success of his mission.

- Continue the actions that are leading to incremental progress.

Disrespecting slow growth will lead to quitting. High expectations and perfectionism kill action and blind you to your own value and contribution. Author of *The Minimalist Entrepreneur,* Sahil Lavingia says brilliantly, "You don't learn, then start. You start, then learn." Continuing what you started leads to smarter action towards growth as you continue what you started.

After over ten years of on and off effort to reach single digit body fat, I finally nailed it a few months ago. I measure in at 9.85%. It meant a lot to me personally. Consistency through every bit of muscle growth and body fat reduction was the key. Simple, but not easy. Some weeks my metabolism stalled and I didn't lose any body fat. But as we tweaked the macro nutrients, adjusted rest days, changed up more aggressive work outs, I would lose another .25% of body fat. The fat burn just eventually added up over more months than I preferred. But I made it.

Listen, this is sure and steady growth. It can be measured. Be encouraged. You're not who you were or where you were.

"Don't compare yourself to anyone but your best self.
It's not about being perfect. It's about progress.
It's about the consistent effort you bring every single day
that leads to small incremental improvements.
Little by little, a little becomes a lot!"
—Rick Godwin

5

Understanding the Value
of Vulnerability

Opportunity Shrouded
by Failure

VULNERABILITY IS UNAVOIDABLE in order to harness adversity for good. With larger than life, brilliant authors and speakers on this subject, I won't attempt to repeat their award-winning content. I'm going to share from a different angle, and offer some wisdom that can hopefully add value as well.

In my opinion and in many successful cases, vulnerability is the number one answer to the questions that many frustrated, angry, broken, and stuck people are asking right now. This includes men who are hurting and men who are hurting both themselves and the ones they love with chronic attitudes and behaviors.

What Is Vulnerability?

I will define this word and what it looks like through-
out this chapter, but first, to provide a baseline, I personally define the word *vulnerable* as *wound-able*. According
to Webster's, vulnerable is made up of two Latin words:
VULNER, to *wound*, and VELLERE meaning to *pluck*.
Webster's, goes on to describe this word as:

1: *capable of* being physically or emotionally
   wounded
2: *open to* attack or damage (…violently with blows
   or words)

Listen, vulnerability is scary, for a number of
reasons. There's no way to Tony Robbin's your way out
of it. Vulnerability is a Goliath! But in part, it's terrifying
because it is not understood for what it really is and how
it can serve.

My Greatest Vulnerability

For the sake of this subject, I think it's important to
set the stage and demonstrate this principle to you myself.

One of my greatest and present vulnerabilities involves an unhealthy behavior of *fear leading to control*. Nothing so much outward, more beneath the surface. And not an aggressive control, more of a behaved control. Yes, more like a structured dysfunction, a slow and clean Vulcan kill.

So, when pressures come at me from multiple fronts, after a while if I'm not staying sharp, I can grow unsettled, uncomfortable, and untrusting on the inside. I can then become heavy-handed on the outside, become a little intimidating with people and a bit of a bully.

It seems over the last couple of years the primary target of this unhealthy, controlling triggered reaction has been toward my two outstanding daughters.

I'm a guy and I'm a dad, and my growing college-age daughters, look like their very beautiful mother. When they were little, I used to be able to love on them, kiss their little faces, make them laugh, make them mad, and tell them what to do, and they would just have no real choice. But children grow up, and as they do, so should some of their personal freedoms. There are certain boundaries for living at home, but there's also the increase of stewarding more of their own personal choices. They can independently taste the benefits of good choices, and the pain of not so good ones.

I wrestle with a toxic fear that they *could* make bad decisions that I *could* not control, and that those consequences *could* possibly alter their future. They *could* hurt themselves, they *could* hurt others, and they *could* hurt their dear dad.

Well, their expanding freedom exposes an old, preexisting condition in my soul: *an internal fear that attempts to bully me with a destructive impulse to control an outcome. I must protect myself from a potentially harmful situation and I must cover myself from the possibility of emotional pain.* In this case, it would be my daughters, "…dating whom I would perceive as the wrong guy, going to the wrong places, watching and listening to the wrong things, over-posting on social media, wearing the wrong clothes, pot, crack, ice, boom, pow."

"You know better! You know the right thing to do! I know the right thing for you to do! I will help you do the right thing!" And here would come the control, critical undertones, and the unspoken disapproval that they could tangibly feel from their dad. This was distancing my daughters from me. *All of these actions are nothing but a faulty form of self-protection from the potential of hurt or disappointment.*

I came face to face with this false belief in my head: "This lie is more important than their freedom to fail."

We can see that their freedom of choice is not the problem, fear is. And now, this problem is creating a problem for others. My reaction is not protecting me or my daughters from attack or damage. So here we are. I am wound-able. I am vulnerable.

Why Men Hate Vulnerability

- One - EGO: an obvious reason and one that's at surface level. We tend to feel we can do it better, and we want to win and dominate. Vulnerability gives off a perceived scent of unacceptable weakness and our *response* is, "I'm gonna change that/fix that/make that right MYSELF! And those that aren't in line will be illuminated with my astounding wisdom on what needs to be done here. Scoot over!"

- Two - FEAR: We can try to pose all we want, but at the end of the day, men dread appearing inferior, getting publicly embarrassed, and are terrified of emotional pain. We rarely face that pain, process that pain, get help for it, and then fail to grow from it. Successful vulnerability seems too elusive, so men often won't engage.

The risk seems too high. We say "no thanks," so we buck up, macho up, bully up; but in reality, we just wimp out, check out, and retreat.

- Three - CONTROL: Just like in my situation. More than control, I say the fear of a lack of control. This brings me to what I believe is the most critical and telling, core description of true vulnerability. It's found in one word: *POWERLESSNESS.*

- A man that is truly vulnerable, *in and of himself,* is helpless. He does not possess the resources to securely protect himself, nor the grace to change himself. By definition he is open and exposed.

- A male's control exposes the stubborn, independent, self-serving, self-protecting, arrogant, egoistic, self-exalting, and ignorant part of human nature. But a prerequisite to vulnerability is accepting your own powerlessness and helplessness against your acutely painful demons, and we loathe this crucible. Pride provokes us to hate dependence and deceives us into isolation and mistrust.

Why Men Should Embrace It

- VULNERABILITY IS YOUR ALLY: Not your enemy. Unhealthy behaviors, controlling desires, and toxic attitudes destroy relationships and erode a man's self-worth. Isolate, see clearly, accept fully, and grow indignant towards your real enemy. These will never somehow be your friend. So, attack and shred confrontations that come with your humanity. Stop with the dread. Sign up for it. Professional fighters know they'll get hit. They volunteer, prepare, and train for it! Conner Mc Gregor didn't wait for his next match. He was negotiating for them. "Yeah, but look at his payday?!" Yeah, and look at yours.

- THE STAKES ARE HIGH: What's at stake (relationships, your business, your sense of value and self-worth, your daughters) deserves our aggressive posture towards vulnerability. *Consider that their success is contingent on our engagement.* My daughter told me, "When you would act angry and untrusting towards me, it made me question if I was going to make the right decisions. I want to do the right thing!" Instead of confidence, I instilled in my daughter self-doubt. Not good. By the way, I hope my vulnerability is helping some of you. That's the idea.

We're built for this, and the stakes are too high not to rise up. Why else should we embrace it?

- POWERLESSNESS LEADS TO POWER: And I'll boldly say, this is what we're after. I want more power. I want more ability. I want to conquer and I want to win. And nothing makes a man feel so small in his soul as being chased off by intimidation. Listen, just because you've spent your own resources doesn't mean help is not available to you. And being "open to attack" doesn't equal being attacked. So be bold, get aggressive and exhaust all your resources so that you can find the motherlode. Push that barbell up until those arms and pecs are shaking, and you can't get that final rep up. You might be tempted to be self-conscious, but the boys that have been there before know this is the key to growth. Get past yourself and know that vulnerability doesn't invalidate you, it qualifies you. It is not preventing your win; it is leading you to do it. On one hand, vulnerability is guiding you towards power, and with the other, you are suffocating the fear that's lying to you.

How Men Can Embrace It

Again, small tweaks lead to big peaks. Now, let's get to what you CAN control. They are actionable. They are measurable. They are doable.

Transparency

You must involve others, and/or a higher power. Because remember: You are powerless to change the circumstances or yourself. You've proven this. Today is not a new day. Your extra cup of coffee didn't change that. No, no. No more habit sanity. Accept this reality. You can't win with your present resources. You're dead.

> *"A leader first and foremost is human. Only when we have the strength to show our vulnerabiltiy can we truly to lead."*
> —Simon Sinek

Transparency means you tell a friend, a counselor, a psychologist, a LMFT, a priest, an individual, a group of people, participate in an AA meeting, a *Celebrate Recovery* gathering, or share with a good listener either in person or by *Zoom* or *Teams* about your broken situation and your vulnerability. Tell your present, sucky story, embarrassing fears, and behaviors. No sugar coating, posing, minimizing, justifying, lying, denying, whether or not you're crying or feel like dying or in hell full-blown frying. Be as straight up and as thorough as you could possibility tell it, spill the details, and confess the genesis. You're going to have to talk, Bruce. Get it out!

Transparency is a CONFESSIONAL action.

Remember guys, we control these actions. USE YOUR WORDS. This is what we used to tell our kids when they were little, didn't we? Well, a lot of us men are like kids in this regard. It's not a put down. It's just an accurate diagnosis. It's arrested development. Men are mute and in an emotional prison, but there is a dynamic, reliable principle we employ when we get out into the light with words what has been ruling our headspace in the dark. It is so simple it takes maturity not to be offended with it. We simply confess our narrative in the presence of another.

As we begin to share, and while hearing our own words out of our mouth in the illuminated setting of others, the inflated details of our situation start to get right-sized. The lies become less scary; the torment, less potent; the fear, less convincing. I also start to recognize my arrogance in this situation, the smallness in my perspective, and seeing how depleted I've become of courage. Somewhere along the way I stopped eating steak and potatoes. Another pair of eyes and ears goes a long, long way.

I've stepped into conversations with someone much wiser and wondered halfway through the third sentence, "I don't really believe what I'm saying right now, do I?" It sounded pathetic. Which leads to this: you must be willing to look and sound foolish. So what? I'd rather face the fear of looking and sounding dumb than pose and lose my daughters. I don't wait to talk until the fear leaves. I talk in the presence of fear, and the power of light will begin to chase it off.

Because....

Transparency about vulnerability creates PROTECTION.

Light is power. It's a defense. It guides to a fruitful path. It exposes traps. It can help heal depression. It emanates warmth. It brings safety.

"Confess your faults to one another, pray for one another, that you may be healed and restored to a spiritual tone of mind and heart" (James 5:16, AMPC).

St. John said confess your faults to God and He will forgive you. St. James says to confess your faults to people and you will be healed. And listen, what you share might not be the catalyst for the life-altering change you're hoping for, but it can be a huge start. Even the small light on the water-ice dispenser on the outside of my refrigerator helps me in the early morning hours to see the coffee pot and pour my coffee into a cup without spilling it on the kitchen counter. Using the normal cell phone light walking downstairs when it's dark can help with safety, because I've fallen down those stairs before for not seeing. So, any small improvement is a major breakthrough when things have been the same dark misery for a long time.

Relationships

Transparency gets your condition OUT there.
Relationship brings someone IN here.

At this level of the HOW-TO, you are willingly to welcome a friend to know you and stay with you in and through your adversity. Often, the person you confess to becomes this relationship in your journey. *Transparency* prepared the soil of your heart for *relationships..*

Your courage will begin to grow, and you'll need this because the cost for a solid friendship in your vulnerability is more than a co-payment for a weekly psychologist appointment. The price is the sacrifice of ongoing exposure to your inadequacies by someone who accepts your imperfections. *Transparency* is ankle-deep risk. *Relationship* is waist-deep risk. That ocean water can almost hurt your feet when you first step in. Wading into waist-deep in the Pacific is another level for brothers no matter what kind of trunks they're wearing. So, while transparency is a confessional action...

Relationships are an INTENTIONAL action.

It demands what I call the three I's: INITIATIVE, INVESTMENT, INVOLVEMENT. You have to initiate because it's not likely to happen by being idle. Again, we control this and we have to own our part. It's an investment and requires your consistent involvement.

The first time I practiced this principle, I fought all kinds of pressure to follow through. I was nineteen and had made a huge, positive shift in my life, but I felt like all of hell was lighting me up in an attempt to get me to go back to the familiar of the old. I sat with this counselor and was determined to spill it all. I knew that he could just tell me I was crazy and walk out of that Pizza Hut, or not.

I walked on water and told him my story, and then was quiet and waited for his response. He said, "GOOD." "Good?" I said to myself while he spoke. He said, "The opposition means that your bold move in the right direction is going to take you great places. You are doing exactly what you need to be doing and the backlash you're facing in your mind and circumstances is evidence you're moving into destiny." As I listened to him speak life to me, with fire coming out of his eyes and fire lighting me up in my heart, I said to myself, "My life will never be the same."

This guy, who counseled me when I was nineteen, is still a reliable friend and sounding board to this day. There's no reward without risk. Some of you risk in business and you're brilliant and successful at it. Pivot that principle towards what we're talking about. This Goliath is measurable and can be sized up.

Relationships IN your vulnerability create ACCEPTANCE.

In the Genesis of human behavior, as we see in the third chapter of the first Book of the Scriptures, a pattern emerges. Fear, control, and blame were clearly displayed in Adam and Eve's reaction following their brokenness. They ran from relationship with their Creator after eating the forbidden fruit. They covered themselves with the faulty protection of fig leaves. They blamed one another, their Creator, and the serpent. I was getting knocked around a bit by the same fear, control, and blame. This is a common pattern. But I realized something more was feeding into this.

I'm convinced that this debilitating force is SHAME. It appears to be a puppet master, a strongman to the rest of the toxic forces at work in human behavior, allying with fear to shield itself. *Shame is distinct and foremost in that it is the only one of these influences that assaults the human identity.* Fear may put us on the run, but shame accuses a valuable human life.

Shame is defined as "to mar, to disfigure and to disgrace." Shame accuses our identity as faulty. It condemns in convincing fashion that one is inferior, less than, and has no place in any community. The Hebrew language describes shame as the "scornful whispering of hostile spectators."

Without taking down shame our quest for successful vulnerability is not possible. It is the master power reigning over the opportunity for healthy vulnerability.

Shame, Job's friend's first cousin once-removed on his mother's side, insinuates:

- You should have known better.
- If you were really a good person you wouldn't have these issues.
- They're not going to accept you if they know.
- It's just like you to fail in this way.
- Something is wrong with you.
- You don't just have problems. You are the problem.
- Look at what you've caused. They'll be better off without you.

At the end of the day shame is telling us: "You are branded as a failure for being vulnerable. You are a marred person due to your weaknesses. Because you are defenseless, you are a disgrace. You are inferior because you deal with a self-defeating behavior. You are truly rejected because you deal with rejection. You are truly a sinner because you've sinned. You are helpless because you need help."

Nah, I just don't buy that anymore. Neither should you. You see, this is where the dynamic principle of relationships demonstrate their effectiveness. Community in vulnerability creates acceptance from others and, therefore, acceptance for yourself. It weakens the assault against your identity for not having it all together. You must allow yourself to be accepted by your community at your worst. You will find that their strength begins to create a separation between shame and vulnerability.

The truth is, vulnerability has everything to do with *not* having it all together. It's what makes us human. This was Paul's driving force behind what he did: a limited human entering into reconciliation with a limitless God, taking the human well beyond his own limitations. We can then see that we are not defined by our condition.

It will take humility and courage to welcome relationships into these places. Humility is the key word. It helps us to get over ourselves, imperfections and all because...

Only LOVE Demonstrated by Acceptance
Drives out SHAME

A classic demonstration of standing up to face vulnerability is Bruce Wayne in *Batman Begins*. Master Wayne was tormented by bats. He was not only attacked by bats, but that fear became connected to the traumatic experience of his parents' untimely death, which he blamed himself for.

> "Even if I am attached, I will remain confident."
> —David, Psalm 27:3

Years later he went back home to Gotham with a clear and more mature mission. As he was deep beneath his estate, a multitude of faithful bats accosted and completely surrounded Bruce. This time, instead of running, panicking, or begging for Alfred's help, he slowly stood up in the middle of his vulnerability with some epic courage. What a great scene!

What was once Batman's greatest fear and trigger of pain, eventually became a canopy of protection *around* him, a weapon *for* him, and a symbol of strength for an entire city. In a similar way, your greatest vulnerability that seemed to lead to your most painful losses, can be transformed into the very shield of defense, a generator of power, and source of hope for you and healing for others.

The very shame, fear, control, and blame that crippled you, can bow its knee to your newfound strength and advantage called vulnerability that was once shrouded by past failures. Lean into this golden opportunity by bringing others into your mess. Their story is your healing. Your story is their healing.

"God gives grace to those who are humble enough
to receive it."
—(James 4:5, AMPC)

6

Understanding the Value of Grace

Multi-force for Multi-problems

"And He said to me, 'My grace is sufficient for you,
*for My **<u>strength is made perfect in weakness</u>**.'*
Therefore, I will all the more gladly glory in my
weaknesses and infirmities, that the strength and power
of Christ (the Messiah) may rest (yes, may pitch a tent
over and dwell) upon me! So now I am glad to boast
about my weaknesses, so that the power of Christ
can work through me."
(2 Corinthians 12:9, NKJV, AMP, NLT)

GRACE IS A free, superhuman, multi-dimensional virtue
that makes you more than your weakness. It is the ability
to take you further and make you more. The more you
experience grace, the less you get in your own way.

Grace is also only at the disposal of those humble enough to receive it, which is why passing the test of vulnerability is required. Weakness is the door leading to strength. Vulnerability is the lock. Humility is the key. Grace is an ability cultivated in an environment of humility. It qualifies us to receive the multi-force of grace to answer life's multi-problems.

A kaleidoscope gives us a different look at the things around us. It turns the ordinary into something dynamic, and something one dimensional into something multi-dimensional. Grace is like a kaleidoscopic. It affects a human heart and is released out and into our world in dynamic and multidimensional ways.

Let's define grace and see what it looks like in weakness:

DEFENSE

Grace protects and defends us when vulnerability makes us a sitting duck. The word "sufficient" from the passage above is from the Greek word *arkeo,* meaning to *raise a barrier and to ward off.* Grace is raising a standard and is a most effective shield.

The word "rest" used in this passage is a key compound word. It can be defined as to superimpose a tabernacle over someone, or to tent upon. *Strong's Concordance* says that it symbolizes to *reside or dwell* (*as God did in the Tabernacle of old, a symbol of protection and communion*). This is the defense that grace freely gives us. You start to feel you're not going to die and that there's some real and reliable help. It says you're okay when you don't look okay, and you actually start to believe it.

SATISFACTION

Grace comes from a word meaning *calm delight.* Grace doesn't excuse people from pressure nor does it erase their problems, but it can nourish and make us content in spite of them. It comes from another world and is welcomed by willing souls to enable them to rest contentedly in their present world. What is this rest and satisfaction worth today? I'd say at least a major stake in the pharmaceutical industry. Grace makes adversity a satisfying meal and contains its own superhuman endorphins.

SUPERNATURAL BRANDING

Strong's defines grace as the "divine influence on the heart and its reflection in the life." Grace brands you. Love and acceptance dominate personal darkness and self-loathing. There is no qualifying behavior to earn it and no useless effort of perfectionism to attain it. There's only the key of humility to unlock the door in order to receive grace and be grateful.

Only when you're dead to self-effort can you be made new. You can then strive from a place of acceptance, not in an effort to earn it. Remember, you can't win. You're spent. Here is where you actually do give up and let go. Divine influence initiates and does the heavy lifting. You get better at receiving.

INFLUENCE

What affects you personally becomes a force that proceeds from you. This divine influence on your heart sparks a reflection coming out of your life. This reflection brings you favor and approval with people.

Grace that enters in translates into a reflection on our countenance that others notice. They may not understand what's going on behind the scenes, but that favor becomes a real currency nevertheless. This reflection is how we add value to others and become selfless in making our world a better place. This influence also favors with a marked likeability factor and brings you before other people of influence.

PARDON

Grace is forgiveness. Yes, the failure is real, and the pain it causes is real. Grace doesn't say otherwise or play it down. Grace is simply more real, on a higher plain, with the ability to release the offender and repair the brokenness.

Grace releases you from reproach. Grace frees you from you. Grace is the only force that can liberate a hurting person from the prison of what I call the "Me" factor. A lot of people can see good things true for others but stumble over the same for themselves. What gets in the way of these things being true for ourselves is the "ME" factor. *I'm a special case. My failure was unique. Other wouldn't reject you but they would me. I won't forgive myself. God's grace is enough for you but I still sense His disappointment in me."* The "Me" factor.

We become willing to let go of our real or perceived role is screwing things up. Yes, it hurt. It's life. We're human. I can't change it. I wish I would have done better. No excuses. Regardless, grace reasons with us, encourages us, shows us it's more advantageous for us, soothes us, and enables us to let go. You've beat yourself up for too long now. It's easier said than done, but go ahead and let grace in and receive pardon.

POWER

Paul's Mentor used the words grace and power inter-changeably when counseling the apostle. Paul needed, experienced. and demonstrated this power effectively and consistently to become the Greatest Salesman in the World. So, just like bacon isn't ever just for breakfast, grace is never only for the forgiveness of sins. It's always been multi-dimensional, and power is a real and acces-sible virtue of it.

In one of his many adventures, Paul was unjustly imprisoned and shipped off to Rome to stand before Caesar but not before enduring an insane storm and shipwreck. He had advised the owner of the ship and the captain to avoid setting sail before winter, but they didn't listen. As a result, all of the cargo was lost. Miraculously, all lives were saved and they ended up on an island called Malta. Paul, still trying to serve, was getting some fire-wood as everyone was still wet and freezing from the ordeal. He was met with a viper fastening its fangs on his arm. What a great few weeks these were! Yet, Grace *satisfied* Paul and he kept going.

Paul shook that viper off of his wrist into the fire. He didn't die. Grace *protected* him. The same people, who accused Paul of being a murderer for getting bitten, were now saying he was a god for not dying. Grace *affirmed* him. Then, the father of the leading Roman citizen of Malta was extremely sick, and Paul prayed for him and he was healed. Soon everyone, including the natives of the island, brought their sick to Paul and he healed all of them. Grace *branded* and *pardoned* these valuable people.

Before leaving Malta, the people honored Paul and supplied all of his traveling needs. Paul headed to Rome on a fancy Alexandrian ship with enough money to rent his own fully furnished house in Rome for two years with no one telling him what to do. Grace *favored* him.

Arkeo, the word for *sufficient,* also means *to avail.* Grace brought Paul *power.* This power advanced Paul as he shredded through adversity with superhuman ability and speed. Grace is not some soft word. It is more than what one needs. Grace is a multi-force for multi-problems.

The root Greek word for grace is *charis,* and connected are the words *chairo* and *chara.* Consider these three closely related words describing grace are used a total of around 260 times in the New Testament. Ashthenia, and its *weakness* related words are used around 42 times. Grace is exercised some six times more than weakness. Grace dwarfs weakness. Where every form of weakness and failure exist, grace superabounds and completely dominates! Grace is the conqueror and weakness is the servant. Grace is enough. Don't hide your weakness, because for *grace to flow, your weakness has to show.*

> *"The weaker we feel, the harder we lean.*
> *The harder we lean, the stronger we grow."*
> (Joni Eareckson Tada)

7

Pressing Into Pressure

Profitable Resistance

But as He went, the multitudes <u>thronged</u> Him. Now a woman, having a flow of blood for twelve years, who had spent all her livelihood on physicians and could not be healed by any, came from behind and touched the border of His garment. And immediately her flow of blood stopped. And Jesus said, "Who touched Me?" When all denied it, Peter and those with him said, "Master, the multitudes throng and press You, and You say, 'Who touched Me?'" But Jesus said, "Somebody touched Me, for I perceived power going out from Me." Now when the woman saw that she was not hidden, she came trembling; and falling down before Him, she declared to Him in the presence of all the people the reason she had touched Him and how she was healed immediately. And He said to her,

"Daughter, be of good cheer; your faith has made you
well. Go in peace."
(Luke 8:42–48, NKJV)

WHEN GRACE BEGINS to get us out of our own way, we start to get more focused about what we want.

This woman was hemorrhaging for twelve years and was considered an outcast by her community. She had exhausted her financial resources and any possibility of a cure. The crowds were so packed that they pressed around the Master. She was a female in a male's world. In spite of this, this woman took the risk, pressed through the pressing crowd, touched the Prince of Peace, and a supernatural force surged from Him like lighting and restored her completely. She pressed into the pressure and demonstrated a pattern we can follow.

Our culture of entitlement, blame, and laziness does not serve to our advantage. Our world is filled with excuses. We'll have to rise above it if we're going to eat the breakfast of champions. Consider that our word *thlipsis* appears in this passage three times, and each occurrence served as a deterrent against this woman's passionate quest to be well again. People were not cheering for her.

She was not at her best in most respects. Same with you and me. However, if she could do it, so can we!

Pressing into Pressure Is Profitable

J. Kip Matthews, Ph.D., a sports and exercise psychologist, wrote a brilliant article on initiating exercise and the reciprocal benefits of brain chemicals such as endorphins, serotonin and norepinephrine. It's too in depth to include the entire article, but this point will do:

It's not just that exercise leads to an increase in serotonin and norepinephrine which may, in turn, reduce depression and stress. Exercise may actually help ward off depression and anxiety by enhancing the body's ability to respond to stressors. What appears to be happening is that exercise affords the body an opportunity to practice responding to stress, streamlining the communication between the systems involved in the stress response. The less active we become, the more challenged we are in dealing with stress.

Exercise then is a controlled and self-induced stressor. It is a practice for life's stresses. So, as we are *proactive* with exercise on our terms, we train ourselves to be less *reactive* out there on the world's terms. Initiating pressure through exercise conditions me for less stress since it generates the healing analgesics of endorphins. Neurotransmitters are inherent natural powers, and I can access them by harnessing the tension of physical training.

I've often stepped onto a stair climber fatigued or frustrated. Yet, after a while I was in a different and much better frame of mind. My renewed sense of encouragement didn't come by a nap (even though they have their place), OR because of an outside change. I simply initiated the tension of exercise and accessed a greater force already programmed in my brain.

It's like participating in a scrimmage to prepare you for the real game. This virtual physical practice is creating stress in our bodies in order to deal with the stress that we already face mentally and emotionally. So, let's create this profitable pressure first!

This woman wanted power from Jesus. But the press, the throng, the people were hiding Him from her. In her uncleanness, in her poverty, abandonment, inner broker image, societal injustice, she responded to the pressure already in front of her. In her own form of resistance, her self-induced pressure separated that crowd enough to get what she wanted and much more. This empowered woman teaches us today that we can also control our growth to some degree and much of our future is in our own hands.

Whether your desired change is walking towards you or away from you, you can initiate movement. In this sense, what is already in you is now greater than what is outside of you.

Unprofitable Resistance

There can come a time when the pressure is too much or unhealthy, making your resistance against it unprofitable. It helps to know when to downshift rather than accelerate. Rest is necessary for healing and recovery, just as pressing is necessary for growth. This can seem like a contradiction and a bit of a moving target, but learning the ebbs and flows of pressure and rest is part of eating the breakfast of champions.

Excessive and unchecked pressure can lead to injury. A brief word study linking our words *pressure* and *vulnerability* show that we can get ourselves in trouble if we do not manage this well.

Thlipsis (*pressure*) comes from the word *thlibo* (*to crowd*). *Thlibo* is from the verb *tribos,* which means, to *rub.* The noun form is defined as a *rut* or a *worn track. Tribos* is from the words *tragos* and *trogo,* which is defined as a *gnawer;* to create *corrosion* or *wear,* to *gnaw* or to *chew.* Interestingly, *trogo* is directly related to the Greek word, *trauma,* or a *wound. Trauma* is related to a primitive root verb *thrauo,* which is defined as to *crush* or *bruise.*

We can't avoid some form of injury when we take risks in a worthy pursuit, but we do want to limit the downsides. One reason it took me so long to get under 10% body fat was because I didn't give myself enough rest when I wasn't feeling well. For one week, I worked out through a mild cold but pushed it too much. My wife and younger daughter warned me, but in my arrogance, I didn't listen. It cost me because the next day I ended up shaking like a leaf with a fever. For the next five weeks, I went from a flu to a hard cold and then to bronchitis. I continued to be weak for another three weeks after. This was unprofitable resistance.

Pressure doesn't always lead to growth. It could lead to a rut, a break down, and serious injury. Listen, depending on the situation, you might need to quit or give up. You could be better off with a necessary ending to that relationship, like Dr. Cloud says. Instead of press, rest. Instead of fasting, eat a piece of cake and laugh. Instead of work, make love to your spouse. Instead of focusing, disconnect and watch a rerun of *Taxi*.

There's a fine line from flowing in your wheelhouse and killing it, to toiling with frustration and killing yourself. That toil can spring from ignorance and pride. It's something to be sensitive to and adjust. This has to do with respecting your present limitations, as well as honoring the process that will lead to the kind of progress you're after.

There have been great moments in sports history where athletes made their mark of greatness as they pressed instead of resting. Willis Reed for the 1970 New York Knicks, Kirk Gibson for the 1988 Los Angeles Dodgers, and Kerri Strug for the USA Women's Gymnastics; these and others will be etched forever in sports greatness for their courage despite injury. They defied conventional wisdom and secured championships and Olympic Gold in a way that inspired tens of millions to this day.

There are rare moments to cross these more risky thresholds of physical and emotional adversity. However, these should be approached with great care, consideration, and with wise insight from others who care sincerely for you.

Simone Biles, considered the greatest gymnast of all time, made an even more courageous move. After landing awkwardly competing on the vault, and citing her battle with mental health, she ultimately withdrew entirely from the 2020 Tokyo Olympics.

"I just think mental health is more prevalent in sports right now…We have to protect our minds and bodies and not just go out and do what the world wants us to do. We're not just athletes, we're people at the end of the day and sometimes you just have to step back," Biles said.

TRUTH. By the way, she endured much more brutal abuse than anything she ever faced in competition. Her wisdom is appropriate for every generation, especially aspiring young adults. SO, from the GOAT-gymnast with over 30 Olympic medals and world championships, all the way to the rest of us, we do well to honor her insight for ourselves.

Admittedly, as a Dodger fan since birth, I would have preferred Gibby win us the Word Series the way he did, even if it meant aggravating his injury ending his baseball career. Selfish? YES. Wrong? Yes. So, listen to your gut, listen to wise counsel. Be wary of the advice of those who are partial to what you do or do not do. Listen instead to the wisdom of those that love you for you.

Playing it smart is not the same as playing it safe. Biles already proved herself a world champion dozens of times over. You're a champion yourself. Don't be bullied into the elephant graveyard by anyone or provoked there by any misguided passion within yourself. We risk in life and eat adversity for breakfast not to attain greatness, but because we already possess greatness.

Keep Peddling

In the summer of 1994, my wife and I had started dating and by then we knew we were going to marry. I finished my A.A. but instead of completing my bachelor's degree, I chose instead to enter into a youth internship to help teens. Had I not, I never would have met my wife. I got a lottery return for that investment. The downside? The uncertainly of my education, career, and the ability to adequately provide for a family was becoming a pretty big mental problem for me.

Soon enough into the relationship, the pressure, insecurity, and grueling attack against my own sense of manhood begin to peak. With no car, I got on my bike, yes my bike, to go to her house to spend time with her family. My wife was then and still is so attractive. I was a 6'2" 170-pound guy who would have weighed in at 150 if it wasn't for my big Mexican head. She could have married anyone she wanted. My future in-laws were loving and accepting for sure.

And here I was: their daughter's knight in shining armor picking her up on my mountain bike for a fancy dinner at Taco Bell while fighting off images of Pee Wee Herman. With each pedal on my way there that Sunday afternoon, I was fighting the trash-talk in my head. I had no food. I had no job. My pets' heads were falling off!

Well, that afternoon I remember vividly coming to a stop sign with still twenty minutes left to get to her house. I stopped, put my head down, feeling all of the weight of this discouragement, seriously wondering if this was going to work or if I was willing to put in the work to mature through this test. In that exact moment, I heard a nearly audible voice say something I will never forget: *"Just keep peddling."*

Listen, I wasn't going to hurt anything by peddling except my pathetic ego. That poser in me needed to die anyways. So then, once you get a clear enough picture of what you're after, you've got to move with intensity. For what it's worth, I don't ride that bike anymore. But I still got that girl.

"Under pressure, you don't rise to the occasion,
you sink to the level of your training.
That's why we train so hard."
—A Navy Seal

8

Grace and Pressure

Dynamic Duo

"For when I am <u>weak</u>, then I am <u>strong</u>."
(2 Corinthians 12:10)

BELIEVING IN OURSELVES can be overrated, especially when there are things about ourselves that we don't like and are self-defeating. Paul was absolutely brilliant, from rich stock and with a most impressive resume before the King met him on the road to Damascus. After that experience, all of his accolades were reduced, giving him this one phrase as his preaching material: "Jesus Christ, and Him crucified." All of his expanded revelation of truth came as a result of this simplified mission. Grace and pressure pruned him in order to change the world.

Grace and pressure can reduce us to our true selves, our best strengths, and core passions. Grace and pressure are the power-twins that break off our perfectionism, the impossible expectations we place on ourselves, and take us into the high places where shame has no oxygen. It filters and tempers us so what remains is a substance that can be built upon. What's left is a purified passion mixed with bold confidence to do great things. Believe in THIS!

Where Is the Win?

Okay, let's be honest. Paul was thrashed often. Why then are we looking to pattern our lives after his and want what he had? Seriously. The Greatest Salesman in the World was a guy who was martyred. And even while alive, Paul was pummeled at nearly every turn. So, where is the win here? Where is the satisfaction, greatness, and power? Where is our motivation and desire to want success in the way he had it? Fair enough. Let's think about this for a sec', Ted.

Yes, Paul was facing serious beatings from a dark, supernatural being. It was the very assignment of this opposing spirit creature: beat up Saul of Tarsus to stop or slow him down. Please understand though, this opponent was taking a far greater beating than Paul was.

Through Paul, one of the seven wonders of the ancient world, the temple of the goddess Diana or Artemis, was brought down. He upended the culture, economics, and religious beliefs of Ephesus to the degree that even one of their own city elders said that Paul was "turning the world upside down." Twelve disciples in Ephesus under Paul's mentoring multiplied so much that this entire region was affected with power by his message. Several million dollars' worth of witchcraft literature became the fuel for a massive bonfire as these new Christ-followers renounced their allegiance to the gods of the Greco-Roman empire. Paul performed unusual miracles. He established works that are named in the *Book of Revelation*. He wrote nearly two-thirds of the second half of the best-selling book in human history. His exploits, contribution, leadership principles, example of personal growth and humility, brilliance, tenacity, and unwavering commitment still live two thousand years later. Paul was the central figure of Og Mandino's book, *the Greatest Salesman in the World*, selling some 15 million copies.

Paul may have been beaten up, but Paul won. Paul may have been beheaded, but Paul won. Paul may have been killed, but Paul lives, so Paul won. Paul told Timothy that he fulfilled his high calling, goal, and mission. Paul won. Foolish exorcists tried to cast out a powerful demon from a man by saying, "I cast you out by the name of Jesus who Paul preaches." The demon replied through the man, "Jesus I know, Paul I know, but who are you?" The possessed man severely beat up those seven brothers and scared the hell out of the people in that territory when they heard the story. Hell knows Paul. Heaven knows Paul. Most in the world today know Paul. Paul won.

A Win Is a Win

Let's all look at the bigger picture. There's been wins. There's been some success. There's also probably been a lot more growth on the inside of us that has yet to affect what's on the outside. Strength on the inside is growth just like growth on the outside is growth. So, more outside growth is coming. It's on the way. It's real progress, and it reflects humility and commitment on your part. Celebrate this win and don't despise it or sell it short.

I would be tempted to belittle my desire to hit single digit body fat for how small-minded it might seem in comparison to how impressive a guy at 5% body at 205 pounds might look. This would minimize what's personally important to us. Remember, this book is about extending beyond our own limitations, not the limitations of others.

When I got sick for those five weeks, it was a familiar type of a setback. For the last ten years whenever I would get close to single digit body fat, some inconvenience would faithfully come up. I would get sick, injured, or would go on vacation and go on a cheat week that turned into a cheat year. My goal would get undermined, and so I simply would not stay consistent.

After talking to my nutritionist that I've been friends with for over ten years, I chose, despite being sick, that I would not retreat this time. Instead of feeling whiney and entitled to go on my In-N-Out eating plan since I wasn't feeling well, I stayed with our plan of macro nutrients. By the time I felt better again after five weeks, I gained less than one percent of body fat. As my body was able, I picked up my weight training, and some HIIT and momentum carried me under that 10% in matter of a few weeks.

I was physically weak, mentally weak, and emotionally weak. But I had been there before. It was familiar. Yet, I knew I was the one with the power of a decision to mix grace and pressure. I received grace for my pride to push when I needed to rest. I then received grace to visualize myself consistent this time as opposed to ten years of voices and defeat reminding me of how I always seem to react to those times of pressure. I received grace in this pressure and took a deep breath to access an ability in me to make me strong where I had proven weakness leading to defeat in the past.

10% body fat doesn't change the world or create something special for a family. However, the principle is the same. A small win is a win. It was my win and it mattered to me. We can pivot wins toward other endeavors with a greater confidence. Grace and pressure develop something in us that wasn't there before and reveal things that were in us we didn't see before.

See the End Game and Win

I'm not a failure for failing. I'm a failure if I never risk in order to be in a position to fail. I'm not a loser for losing. I'm a loser if I never step up to the plate and swing in order to strike out.

I love watching documentaries and clips of great women and men who have created remarkable organizations and championed great change. We tend to revel only in the end product without absorbing the cost of their constant setbacks to get there. Our head goes quickly to the last chapter of success and the walk-off in the bottom of the ninth inning. But our hearts are enlarged when we see their impossible odds. They found a way and paved a way for us to do the same.

There is no strength without weakness. There is no tree of life without hope deferred. There is no treasure without pressure. There is no character without adversity. Consequently, since adversity and pressure is the breakfast of champions, go enjoy your next meal!

*"Do not fear the people of the land, **FOR THEY ARE OUR BREAD**. Let's go up at once to take the land. We can certainly conquer it!"*
(Joshua and Caleb, Numbers 14:9, 13:30)

Printed in the USA
CPSIA information can be obtained
at www.ICGtesting.com
JSHW022200120324
59030JS00004B/160